Grateful for Grandpas

Written & Illustrated by Jean Forsythe

Dedicated to:

My husband, Dave Forsythe,

A wonderful Grandpa

Grandfathers are special men who go by many names. Whether you call yours Pops or Grandpa, you love him just the same.

There is Gramps, Papaw and Grandad, Pampaw and Grampy too. No matter what you call him, he loves you through and through.

He gives us rides
Up on his shoulders,
On backs,
And sometimes
On his knee.

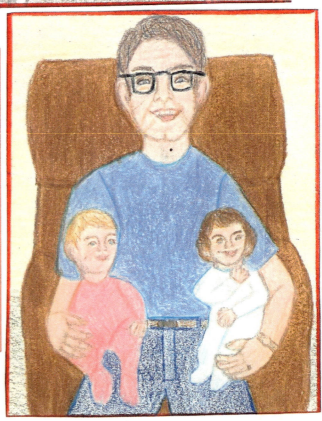

Although he may be busy,

He always has the time for tea.

When Grandpa colors with me,
He always stays inside the lines.

But he likes my pictures best.

He thinks blue skin and green hair look just fine.

Grandpa can fix
Broken toys
Or bandage our
Skinned knees.

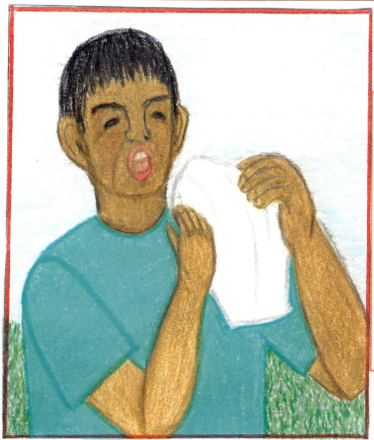

He helps us
Celebrate birthdays,

And says,
"God bless you,"
When we sneeze.

He is there for our school programs

And to watch us play our games.

He takes us out for special treats,
And he calls us silly names.

**Grandpa is good at reading stories,
And sometimes he makes up his own.**

He can act real goofy with us.

He tells bad jokes that might make us groan.

He plays peek-a-boo and tic-tac-toe -

And almost always lets us win.

And whenever we play doctor,
He lets us operate on him.

He can never find us when we play hide and seek.

And when we lie down for a nap, he's always first to fall asleep.

Grandpa helps us build things -

And even teaches us to fish.

He pushes our swings high as the sky –
We almost fly... or so we wish.

I polish Grandpa's fingernails.

He lets me style his hair.

And when I put his make-up on,

His beauty is quite rare!

He crawls inside my blanket fort,

Although he does not fit.

He finishes my ice cream cone,

When I am done with it.

I help him with the gardening.

Together we pull all the weeds.

Whenever we eat watermelon,
He shows me how to spit the seeds

When we splash in the bathtub,

He doesn't mind if he gets wet!

He mops up all the water,

And he doesn't even get upset.

He helps me learn to ride my bike.

He walks me to the park.

He lets me cuddle, really close,
When stormy skies are very dark.

He takes me to the swimming pool and helps me learn to swim.

He takes me many places.
I love to see new things with him!

He takes me out for junk food,

And sometimes steals my fries.

He dances ballet with me.

(The tutu isn't his size.)

He sometimes plays video games with me -

After I show him how to play.

When pajamas are on and stories read,

He bows with me,
And then we pray.

He sings with us,
He laughs with us -
He loves us good or bad.

There's nothing like a grandpa's hug
When we are feeling sad!

No matter what you call yours,
No matter where you live,
Grandfathers are our treasured past,
With so much love to give.

If you believe your grandfather is one of the very best,

Gives yours an extra special hug for you are truly blessed!

The End

Made in the USA
Columbia, SC
05 June 2020